HERBIE · KNOTT

BLACK AND WHITE

HERBIE · KNOTT

BLACK AND WHITE

Boxtree

For EVA KNOTT

First published in the UK 1990 by BOXTREE LIMITED,
36 Tavistock Street, London WC2E 7PB

1 3 5 7 9 10 8 6 4 2

Sources of quotations:
page 35 Lord Wilson, *The Independent*, 11 June 1987
page 61 The Dragon, *The Sunday Times*, 7 March 1982
page 85 Anthony Quayle, *The Independent*, 9 March 1988
page 86 Shirley Conran, *The Sunday Times*, 23 October 1983
page 93 Clive James, *Honey*, July 1985
page 97 Dolly Parton, *The Independent*, 2 April 1983
page 108 Robert Maxwell, *The Sunday Times*, 13 May 1990

Designed by Dave Goodman and Paul Cook/Millions Design.
Typeset in Linotron Univers Condensed by Tradespools Ltd, Frome.
Colour reproduction by Fotographics, Hong Kong.
Printed and bound by Wing King Tong, Hong Kong.

British Library Cataloguing in Publication Data
Knott, Herbie
    Black and white: the photographs of Herbie Knott.
    1. English photographs
    I. Title
    779.0942

ISBN 1-85283-283-5

CONTENTS

FOREWORD

Herbie Knott has regularly contributed photographs to *The Independent* since the newspaper was founded in the autumn of 1986. His lucid, witty images have been part of the process of redefining the role – I would say power – of photographs in a daily newspaper. The truth is that still, black and white pictures can have as much emotional power as moving, coloured images in television. Newspaper photographs may be comment, decoration or an entire point of view. They are as valuable as words. They can be serious, or fun, or anything in between. Just as a newspaper writer's work may rise to the level of art, so may the output of a newspaper photographer. You may collect paintings or you may collect photographs, for both engage the same skills, excite the same pleasures. Turn these pages for the proof of that.

Andreas Whittam Smith, Editor, *The Independent*

BLACK AND WHITE

Fleet Street has changed out of all recognition in the fifteen years since I shot the first of the photographs in this book. The physical change, the movement of newspapers away from the old EC4 ghetto, is obvious. Only a luddite sentimentalist could mourn the scruffy, squalid offices in the shadow of St Paul's, or the idiocy of attempting to shift millions of copies of newspapers from a network of streets so cramped that it required truck-driving of rare genius to negotiate newsprint deliveries down alleyways designed for a horse and cart. The London papers were scarcely read in parts of Scotland. They arrived a day late, with luck. Sometimes they didn't arrive at all, for strikes were endemic, the legendary restrictive practices of the print unions combining with bull-headed management to ensure a fitful stream of stoppages. The process culminated in the closure of *The Times* and *Sunday Times* in 1978, and their subsequent purchase by Rupert Murdoch. The business would never be the same again.

The production process was as Victorian and primitive as anything seen today in the Communist museum of Eastern Europe. On the editorial floor at the *Evening Standard* in Shoe Lane, photographs and messages whizzed backwards and forwards on an overhead-wire system which snapped and rattled as the spring-loaded missiles went on their way. It could have been designed by Heath Robinson. Typesetting, in hot metal, on ancient composing machines arranged in long, dark, Kafkaesque lines, belonged to the age of Caxton. Above all it was an immensely noisy profession, the rumble of the presses reverberating through the building, combining with the rattle of composing machines, the crashing and thumping of platemakers, all filtering up to the editorial floor where a deafening cacophony of shouting and typewriters filled the air, requiring a singularly determined level of concentration on the part of the writers to get anything done at all. It was romantic, and exciting, and unbelievably inefficient. Yet it was still possible to get a picture onto the front page of the *Standard* within twenty minutes of shooting it. A few prayers, two-minute developer, methylated spirit and a cigarette-lighter to dry the negative saw to that.

Photographers were in many ways regarded as a necessary evil. Then, as now, there was a habit of appointing picture editors who did not always understand what they were looking at. The reason for doing this was because the senior editorial staff did not always understand photographers, and would rather discuss things with someone with whom they felt they could communicate, than risk an impenetrable conversation with the journalistic equivalent of a Martian. Thus, on his first morning as picture editor of the *Evening Standard*, Philip Evans was presented with a lot of small 35mm contact prints, over which he waved a magnifying glass with an apparent air of authority. Then he was given some rather larger 6cm by 6cm contact prints, fresh out of chief photographer Aubrey Hart's battered and beloved Rollei. 'Ah!', said Evans, perking up instantly. 'These are *very* clear. Why can't I have them all this size?' But, despite his obvious handicaps – and he never really attempted to master the intricacies of which bit of kit does what – he was successful in the job. He had an instinctive nose for a story, and having dispatched his troops on their missions, let them get on with it. He later became the *Standard's* news editor, probably with a huge sigh of relief.

The tabloids were changing rapidly, thrashing about from one approach to another to try to escape the onslaught of ever-more-efficient television news-gathering, and they quickly became sterile ground for any kind of traditional photo-journalism. On the big occasions – the terrible disasters, the great trials, the royal weddings – they would use pages and pages of pictures, and still do. But from day to day their picture content shrank away to a dreary parade of celebrity snaps and television-related stories, interspersed with Page Three girls. Things weren't much better elsewhere. The *Sunday Times* stood out like a beacon, with Harry Evans' insistence that pictures could tell their own story, often unrelated to the surrounding copy, and with the humblest photographer meticulously by-lined to ensure recognition for his or her work. Frank Herrmann, Sally Soames, Michael Ward, Peter Dunne, Bryan Wharton, Duncan Baxter and Chris Smith produced a stream of immaculately crafted images. *The Observer*, too, used its pictures well, the work of Jane Bown, Eamonn McCabe, Tony McGrath and Neil Libbert outstanding. But elsewhere, newspaper photography was becoming a grim desert.

NOW! magazine was a welcome change, and an heroic failure. In many ways it was a precursor of the new-technology newspapers which have followed since, started from scratch, operating from modern offices. There was a fresh, enthusiastic, family air about the office, and a greater integration of the picture desk into the day-to-day planning than anywhere else except, perhaps, the *Sunday Times*. The photographers did much of their own editing, and would often be found doing so way into the night, fired up by their new-found sense of involvement, and the welcome responsibility that went with it. At its best, the results were spectacularly good. But the publisher, Jimmy Goldsmith, ran into financial problems elsewhere in his empire, and though the flagging circulation had begun to turn the corner, it was too late to save the loss-making magazine. The shutters came down with a thump one Monday morning in April 1981.

By 1986 I was sufficiently fed up with the whole business to have picked up the telephone to enquire about entry requirements to the National Film School. I had always enjoyed working with film crews, and had massive admiration for the skill and craft of British film technicians. Then I received a call from Arthur Foster, who was assembling a team to work at *The Independent*. Mike Crozier, in overall charge of the newspaper's design, had compiled a list of potential photographers, and, having worked with me at *NOW!*, he had included my name. When I walked into the near-empty office to see Arthur, Andreas Whittam Smith was working at a nearby desk. He looked up, nodded, and smiled. The omens seemed encouraging.

It was chaos to begin with. We had no darkroom and took our films to a borrowed photographer's studio half a mile way, where Peter Gillard, our sole printer, looked puzzled when I asked him to 'push' a couple of films. 'What's that?', he asked, bemused. 'Oh, just leave them in the developer too long', I replied, or words to that effect. 'You sure?', said Peter, before I stomped off to complain that we seemed to be employing infants and orphans. The complaint was misplaced. Peter became the best darkroom printer I have worked with, and one of the funniest, producing a non-stop stream of execrable, unprintable humour that would even get photographer Jeremy Nicholl laughing on one of his bog-Irish Black Dog days when he sometimes vented his wrath on the darkroom walls. A steady stream of carpenters was kept busy patching them up, muttering darkly about the increasingly unlikely excuses.

Arthur Foster was replaced before launch by Alun John, and he and Mike Spillard, in cahoots with Chris McKane, the depty home editor, inveigled our pictures into the paper with projection that was revolutionary for 1986. Picture use had been steadily diminishing elsewhere, and the open pages of the early issues of *The Independent*, which carried relatively few advertisements, provided a ready canvas. There had never been any deliberate intention to make *The Independent* a picture-led newspaper, though the clean design of the pages and superb reproduction, begged good picture usage. But the readers' response, in unsolicited letters and through marketing research results, produced such positive feedback that it became policy. Looking back four years later to the early issues it seems odd that the feedback should have been so strong. Picture use throughout the paper is so much better now than it was then. As much as anything else, it reflected how awful standards were elsewhere. But Andreas was quick to see the potential, and, for one whose background lay in the gloomy, austere world of the old *Telegraph* building, where photographers were a species you did not mention in polite company, he became a rapid

and enthusiastic convert to the joys of seeing pictures given room to breathe. He has remained an enthusiast ever since.

The pictures in these pages contain no images of disaster, nor of riot or strife. Although I have photographed my fair share of turmoil, and tragedies such as the Clapham rail crash, they do not belong in the mainstream of my work in the past fifteen years, and I find them curiously remote and unappealing. They are a part of life, and of journalism, but they are not central to it. They are, in a sense, things that happen to people, rather than things that people do for themselves, and the latter are almost always more interesting, curious, and amusing. I have included the pictures of the Kurds, and of Polisario, because I admired their guts and resilience in adversity, and the picture from Ethiopia, because the tranquil, almost biblical setting, was so at odds with the reality of the situation. *Black and White* is a collection of my own passions, of people whose company I have enjoyed, or who have intrigued me. It also contains a few of the steam engines I spent hours watching as a child, and a few of the vintage aircraft I read about in *Biggles*, and spent entire lessons doodling on the back of an exercise book when I was supposed to be reading Caesar's *Gallic Wars* before breakfast at Clevedon House, my Yorkshire prep school. The headmaster, Frank Kidson, was a First World War ace.

The library there was stuffed with childhood joys. As well as a complete collection of Biggles (over 100 books), there was Bulldog Drummond, Rider Haggard, Buchan, Henty, T. E. Lawrence, and a host of lesser derring-do. I developed my first film there, in a little darkroom next door to the carpentry shop in the cellar. I could not have imagined then that the combination of the books I read so avidly and the little cardboard Coronet camera my father had bought on the way home from watching Cyril Washbrook score a duck for Lancashire, would one day combine to send me travelling across Africa. The camera was the means, but the reason was the adventure, and, hand on heart, I defy any journalist to deny it. We do this job because we enjoy it, and those who don't enjoy it don't stay doing it for long. It is a passion, or it is nothing.

At its best, it is also a job where humour is never far from the surface, for humour is an essential part of the human condition. Just before I settled down to write this introduction, David Marsh, Sheffield United fan, and, in his work-breaks, *The Independent*'s night editor, gave me the perfect tailpiece. Shouting across to the Picture Desk he asked, 'Have we got a picture of this second mad cat? The one in Belfast?' Then, after a moment, he added, 'Just a head and paws will do'.

Some things never change.

RAINY DAYS AND SUNDAYS

Wet Night in Brighton
1 May 1988

The South Downs came in view, "Those are the hills that separate Worthing from civilisation," Herbie Knott said. We were driving down the A24 from London, under orders to discover how and why the louts who drink in order to get blind drunk behave as they do, and confident of the kind of story we would find:

THUGS IN BANK HOLIDAY RAMPAGE

The seaside town of Worthing was terrorised yesterday by gangs of drunken youths who roamed through the streets wielding bottles, knives and iron bars. . .

Having dealt with the "facts", which Mr Knott would render even more horrifying by taking a picture of young Englishmen beating up innocent passers-by, the article would offer an "analysis". The youth of today, it would be said, deliberately drinks to excess. He then behaves in the most barbarous fashion. If towns like Worthing are to be saved, young men will have to be kept away from alcohol. There would be nothing in the "analysis" to which the Temperance League could object. It would be written in the responsible tone which British puritans usually adopt.

The relief of finishing one's story before going to see something is considerable. As Sydney Smith might have said, examining a subject prejudices a man so. Mr Knott and I stopped for dinner.

We continued afterwards to Worthing, left our bags at an hotel on Marine Parade and reached Montague Street just before the pubs closed. I had been assured that at this time on a Saturday night, and particularly on a bank holiday weekend, Montague Street would fill with yobs and fights might start. But although there were many people about, neither Mr Knott nor I thought the situation looked promising.

In the Fountain pub, young people were drinking in what can only be described as a deplorably unthreatening manner. They were drinking because it is fashionable. A barmaid told me that the Carioca Disco, where I had intended to go later, was "too young" for me. She recommended Bubbles.

Two policemen entered. They proceeded to the back of the pub, while a number of the youngest drinkers hurried to the door. A youth from Lancing told us the officers were checking whether an extension had been granted to stay open until 11.30pm. They left, satisfied by the papers the landlord had produced.

Bubbles, which claims, ambitiously, to be "Worthing's No. 1 Nite Spot", is just round the corner from the Fountain. On the door we found a notice: "Over 21's – Smart Dress Only – No Jeans, T-shirts,

cord jeans, trainers – 8.30 till late – the Management Reserve the Right of Admission."

A bouncer peered through a small barred window at us. "No," he said. It was starting to rain. Once some other customers had left, we were let in. We paid £3 a head and found ourselves in a dark room with a bar, flashing lights reflecting off mirrors, and disco music. Thanks, perhaps, to the vigilance of the bouncers, there seemed no chance of a fight. We started to talk to two girls, one dressed in black, the other in a colour identified by my companion as "condom pink".

Mr Knott had yet to find a single subject worthy of the small camera he had concealed about his person. "There's nothing for it," he said. "We'll have to dance." The girls refused.

"I'm going to Brighton," I said, embarrassed to have wasted Mr Knott's time. He sportingly agreed to accompany me. By the time we found a taxi we were quite wet.

In Brighton, 11 miles to the east, the first sight we saw was of a man flying at speed out of the side of a building. He had been thrown out of Busby's, a disco just along the front from the Grand Hotel, where in 1984 the IRA tried to murder the Cabinet. The man kicked at the door and abused the bouncers in vain. As in Worthing, plenty of policemen were in evidence. We were admitted to Busby's, but only after showing a press card. "You can tell you're in a bigger city," Mr Knott said. "The sound system's better. The girls are prettier." We split up. I asked a girl what Brighton was like. "Boring," she said.

"There are some nice girls here," a man warned me. "But there are plenty of guys who can't twig. They're the ones you've got to watch."

"Is there much trouble here on bank holiday weekends?" I asked.

"Oh no, it's bad every Saturday," he said, in the voice of one wishing it to be understood that Brighton lads could create their own trouble.

"Get out of her pants and into her bra," the disc jockey said introducing a Billy Ocean song which runs, "Get out of my dreams and into my car." Some couples were nearly copulating. But many more of the girls, while looking stylish, were keeping their distance from the men. Many wore black skirts ending several inches short of black stockings which reached just above the knee.

The disco started to close at 2am. We went out into the rain. A man was peeing in the street. There were one or two near-fights, but many policemen on hand to intervene if they could not avoid it. Most striking was the good humour of the long taxi queue we joined. Nobody was dressed for cool, wet, blustery weather, but laughter predominated. The picture which accompanies this article is of a scene on the other side of the street to the queue.

"We don't want pictures," a youth shouted at Mr Knott. "We want ****ing umbrellas." I like people who understand that it is possible to be insulting and friendly at the same time.

After nearly an hour in the rain, we got a taxi. The driver was a monstrous character. Observing that we were still single, he told us about a club he used to visit. "I always used to pull something round about 20 [years old] there. Even when I was 40, I was still pulling them. Especially the students in the summer." His second wife is from the Mediterranean. "They'll always look after you," he said of her countrywomen. "The only thing is they start off thin and then they get a little bit lumpy. Luckily I managed to find a woman without any inhibitions at all. Mind you, I've found a few."

If we had hunted for long enough in Brighton, or even Worthing, we would have found trouble. The current issue of the *Worthing and West Sussex Evening Argus* contained reports of two appalling attacks on women, an 81-year-old in Crawley and an 18-year-old Argentinian language student in Hove. I was told of a club near Worthing which some taxi-drivers refuse to visit, while others keep a large spanner or wrench to hand when they go there. Bank holiday Mondays on Brighton beach have a bad reputation.

At breakfast on Sunday, I asked one of the waiters whether bank holiday trouble was common in Worthing. "You don't get much here," he said. "I run a burger bar. I was up until five o'clock this morning. You see loads of drunks but you never get any trouble." "We get 30 or 40 bikers some evenings," he said. "They all drink cups of tea, with two sugars very often; sometimes three. They're very polite."

A pretty maid who was cleaning the bedrooms told me: "The rowdy lot we get here are the 18-30 lot. You know how they are. They get drunk and have a good time. But we haven't had any serious violence. We have the occasional fights in pubs on Saturday night."

I do know the Club 18-30 lot. My previous editor sent me on holiday with them to Majorca. Their curious custom is to drink past the vomiting stage, but in vain I asked the Majorcans running the hotel whether they didn't detest the resulting rudeness of their British visitors. For the most part, the people in Arenal, near Palma, seemed as tolerant of drunken high spirits as the waiter and maid in Worthing.

Before leaving town, I saw an advertisement for an event at the Pavilion, where Big Daddy is to take on Raslin' Rasputin. Further down the bill, Bearman Elijah, "Walthamstow bear-hug specialist", will wrestle with Karl Krammer, "hard-hitting tough guy". Sometimes, I think, the reports we read about our appallingly drunken and violent society are as exaggerated as these gentlemen may prove tomorrow night.

(Text by Andrew Gimson © *The Independent*)

**The packamac chorus line –
American football at Wembley**
31 July 1988

Jonathan Foster, *The Independent* sports writer, was entranced by this lot. He saw little of the game: the girls were taller than he is.

They boost the lads' morale in times of trouble, though the overall effect is not the Royal Ballet: it's a sort of giant, shrink-wrapped, clockwork-hamster chorus.

They should be hired for Test Matches. When the West Indies are batting.

**Nuns in a hurry to see
the Pope at Roehampton**
29 May 1982

An awesome spectacle, a bit like a religious version of Leeds United on tour. They poured across the rope barriers and swamped the Popemobile. There was an air of sexual ecstasy about the occasion – and all this before breakfast.

Dennis Todd arrives at his wedding by parachute

Not much of a navigator, our Dennis. He fluttered down from the sky and missed the church by half a mile, landing in the middle of a cricket match. But a passing taxi came to the rescue, whilst his bride Ingrid King waited patiently for him. The Rev Henry Burgin did the honours at All Saints, Blackheath.

Diana, Sally and Susie at Anna's wedding

Diana Van der Klugt, Sally Henderson and Susie Swan were at a wedding in West Sussex two weeks earlier. They did not try parachuting.

25 May 1985

16

11 May 1985

Kevin takes a snap at Annie's wedding, West Sussex
5 September 1987

Annie Henderson married Anton Mitchell in September 1987. Anton did not parachute to his wedding. He was smart, and went by car.

Kevin flies aeroplanes better than he takes snaps. First Officer Faint is a Britannia Airways co-pilot. His wife, Carrol, once threw a bucket of water over me at 2 am. We were flatmates, and my typewriter was keeping her awake.

Nicholas Henderson, aged two, was just a glint in his mother's eye, albeit rather a large one, in the previous picture.

Oxcentrics on the Cherwell
A picnic at Henley

The passion for enjoying the summer. A sodden lot at Henley making the most of half a crate of champagne in the car park, and stuff the rowing. Adrian Sheen, standing, in boater and punt, was whooping it up with his superb jazz band on the Cherwell in 1976. They lashed two punts together and filled the air with lovely, ragged Dixieland on a memorable afternoon. His advertising career was never like this.

June 1976

June 1989

Stewards' enclosure, Henley
4 July 1985

The conversation.

Umbrellas

The man in the deckchair was a museum director, listening to the Central Band of the RAF in the last concert of the summer, in St. James's Park, London. *The Times* used the snap on the front page the next day, 17 September 1975, the first photograph I had published in a national newspaper. They paid £9.60, about the same price as the replacement for the pair of shoes I was wearing, which fell apart at the seams on the way out of the building.

My umbrella-man died in the late 1970s or early 1980s, but not before he had walked into a guest room at Merton College, Oxford, for a conference, and seen the same picture of himself on the wall. Later, he met my sister, then a picture restorer, in Moscow, and befriended her. She sent him a postcard to thank him for his help with this and that. Once again, it bore the same photograph.

16 September 1975

The BBC strikers were having a damp and rather genteel rally on Shepherds Bush green in West London. The lips remind me of the lady with the cigarette-holder in the Osbert Lancaster cartoons. For me, the picture underlines Lancaster's supreme ability as an observer of the British. The difference between us is that he had seen and used that poised and funny certainty in his drawings. I picked it up by sheer accident. I did not see the lips at the moment I shot the picture.

But then, I suppose you make your luck. I had dogged the same girl half-way round the green. She was a drama producer.

24 May 1989

Roy Mason catches a trout
2 June 1987

One of those lovely, heavy June days, when the rain is warm and gentle and the trees whisper under the weight of their leaves. I borrowed a boat and rowed out to meet him, but he didn't get any bites, and decided to go back for lunch. He trolled a line as he rowed to shore, and then leapt in delight to land his first fish of the day. Out of sight, on the bank, his detectives kept watch. Former Northern Ireland Secretaries are guarded for life.

Allan Lamb turned up to try his luck before I left. The rain had washed out his match against Kent, and he sped from the county ground to enjoy his unexpected leisure.

22 July 1987

22 July 1987

The Queen's Prize at Bisley

One up the spout, Matilda?
Bisley is a delightful shambles of rotting clubhouses filled with fading snaps of the lions of 1910. The Mecca of rifle shooting, it staggers along on a shoe-string, giving pleasure to the thousands who have the calm nerves to compete. The ladies have their own trophy in the Queen's Prize competition. It is called the Amazons' Cup.

The Range Officer was an Army dentist, somewhat miffed at being caught with his huge ice-cream. He'd been lecturing the chaps on the evils of sugar-filled foods.

Belfast
14 July 1988

Walking the dog

Ulster

Belfast is a fascinating, beguiling city in which to work, full of unexpected encounters, and some of the most friendly, amusing and likeable people anywhere in the world. It is a hospitable city in a way which has been forgotten elsewhere in the United Kingdom, which only serves as a counterpoise to the tragedy of a divided community. Driving back into it at dawn, with the sun rising over the Lough, it is a setting of such stunning, breathtaking beauty, that you cannot imagine why the smell of fire from a night's rioting should still haunt you.

Ulster has been ill-served by politicians, both Irish and English, for hundreds of years. But the people of the Province just get on with leading their lives. They do it with patience, with humour, and with love.

The sleeping loyalist was at Keady in Co. Armagh; the Catholic mother and child in New Lodge, Belfast.

16 July 1989

12 July 1989

Lawson, Parkinson, Biffen, Wilson

Nigel Lawson was in the garden at No 11, Downing St, which was just as well, because his own usually looked like a jungle. Cecil Parkinson was at home in Hertfordshire, and looking forward to his Sunday lunch. John Biffen probably wasn't, because he had just lost his job as Leader of the House.

3 October 1987

Lord Wilson, campaigning in Huddersfield, seemed unconcerned by any wider political canvas, preferring to show his 1923 Huddersfield Town cigarette cards to anyone who cared to have a peek. 'Look, look, there's Harold Macmillan', shouted one excited woman, grabbing her husband. 'He's dead now, you know,' came back the Wilson reply.

10 June 1987

August 1981

Brighton

A hazardous business, photographing on the naturist
beach at Brighton. They have a habit of throwing stones
at you, and quite right too. So what does the wise
photographer do? He takes his clothes off. All of them.
And he remembers the sun-tan cream. Inelegant,
maybe, but it works.

September 1983

24 March 1984

Feeding time

The joys of a school outing in the rain, and the patience of age.

But don't be misled by those angelic old faces. Chelsea Pensioners are murder to photograph. They have the politician's unerring ability to spot a camera at 100 paces. The Royal Hospital's Ceremony of the Christmas Cheeses dates from 1691. The Hammersmith Cub Scouts were on a Zoo Quest at London Zoo, and spent at least as much time jumping in puddles as they did looking at the animals.

2 December 1987

LADIES
PLAYERS
ONLY

**'Sir' Geoffrey Boycott
at Weston Super Mare**
12 August 1982

'Sir' Geoffrey – arguably the greatest English batsman since W.G. Grace – was doing his bit signing autographs on a gentle, summer's eve at Weston Super Mare. He'd been playing in the same team as Ray Illingworth, whom I'd been dispatched to photograph for the *Sunday Times*, for a Mike Brearley profile.

The legal World Cup
13 September 1987

Lawyers are natural cricket-lovers, if only because the game is a contemplative pastime for spectators, and its rules are labyrinthine. Sir Roy Beldam, a High Court judge, was umpiring; a solicitor, Jim Arnott, doing the medium-pace trundling.

As Martin Johnson, *The Independent*'s cricket correspondent, and wit, once observed, given the right wicket, a ball with a big enough seam, and a bit of luck, you could employ two gatemen at random, and the wickets would fall like ninepins.

But, on this occasion, the batting wasn't up to much.

Castle Rising v. Italy
15 August 1987

The Italians relied heavily on a contingent with roots in the Sub-Continent for this crunch encounter in deepest Norfolk, but they were confounded by Castle Rising's secret ingredient, the three members of the Ellis family.

Ellis v. Italy was no contest. Italy batted first, achieving a total of 47, fuelled by copious quantities of *birra Peroni*. Then Castle Rising – AKA Ellis United – went in for the kill. It was all over in a flash. Castle Rising won by 10 wickets.

Afterwards, there was surprisingly little bad feeling. Both sides got drunk. It was all quite different from my last competitive hockey game, played in Paris, for a scratch touring side from Wimbledon. Someone scythed somebody else after about one minute. Then somebody scythed someone back. Five minutes after the start, all 22 players were sent off for collective misdemeanour. I can't remember who won in the end, but it was good fun.

After the Castle Rising match, the Italians were rethinking their future touring plans. Iceland, perhaps?

Harry's game
26 March 1986

David 'Harry' Bassett played only 35 league games in the Fourth Division, but as a football manager he became a legend. In the 1980s he took poverty-stricken Wimbledon all the way from the Fourth Division to the First, and then did it all over again elsewhere between 1988 and 1990, rebuilding a demoralised Sheffield United team in the Third Division, reaching the First with promotion in successive seasons.

His style was the antithesis of cheque-book management. An intuitive tactician, he sought players who would work for each other. His Wimbledon team became known as 'The Crazy Gang', and were written off by critics as bargain-basement hoofers. But seven of them went on to win varying levels of international recognition by 1990.

Wimbledon achieved First Division status in a blood-spattered game at Huddersfield in May 1986. In the thunderstorm that washed down the Chernobyl fallout, Lawrie Sanchez, bought for £15,000 for a Third Division promotion push, scored the goal that mattered. Glyn

Hodges (R), soon to play for Wales, and Mark Morris (L), ran to congratulate him. Alan Cork, who scored over 140 goals in all four divisions, danced a jig in the background.

Sanchez later represented Northern Ireland, and went on to score the goal that won the FA Cup for Wimbledon in 1988. Mark Morris took to the promotion trail a second time as the lynchpin of Sheffield United's defence. When Sheffield went up to the First, thrashing Leicester City 5-2 on the last Saturday of the 1989-1990 season, Bassett was congratulated in a Commons motion tabled by the city's MPs.

Watching Bassett training his Wimbledon team in Germany in 1986, an army colonel told me that he was one of the best natural leaders of men he had ever seen. 'We have yards and yards of books to tell us how to do that sort of thing. Bassett hasn't read any of them, but he still knows more about leadership than any of us.'

His nickname came from his father, who was called Harry. As a child he was dubbed 'Little Harry', and it stuck.

31 December 1989

7 May 1987

Mother gun (pages 48–9)
24 May 1990

Pete Flynn and Jonathan Elwes

Stanley Mann was enjoying himself at Milbrook Circuit in May 1990, in the 6½ litre Bentley-Jackson which dates from 1926. It was nearly broken up for spares in the 1960s before being rescued from oblivion by Vaughan Davis, whose friends told him he was mad. Thirty years later it is capable of over 140mph, and if it ever went to auction the price would be well over a million pounds. It's called Mother Gun.

Pete Flynn, former British Airways jumbo pilot, developed this strange flying machine, for both military and pleasure use. Powered by a small engine, his 'Powerchute' can rise to around 10,000 feet. On trial runs, his dog follows.

Jonathan Elwes took me flying in his Tiger Moth in May 1987. He later flew to Moscow and back. He was the first Western light aircraft pilot to fly to Moscow since Matthias Rust unexpectedly dropped in on Red Square, terminating several Soviet defence chiefs' careers. Jonathan, sensibly, asked permission first.

**Mark Hanna and
Stephen Grey at Duxford**
6 June 1980

Put these two anywhere near a Second World War fighter aircraft and you find out what flying to the limit is all about. Mark Hanna is a former RAF Phantom pilot who works with his father at Duxford. Stephen Grey's Fighter Collection, based a few hangars away from the Hannas, restores and maintains another large collection of vintage aircraft. Both are used to filming, and flew in *Piece of Cake*. Their other screen credits include *Empire of the Sun*, and *Southern Belle*. Hanna flew the Messerschmitt Me109, chased across the airfield by Grey's Spitfire.

Ray Hanna at Charlton Park
15 November 1987

Ray Hanna was test-filming for the LWT television series *Piece of Cake* in November 1987. A former leader of the Red Arrows, and originator of many of their most spectacular manoeuvres, he now runs the Old Flying Machine company at Duxford. The Spitfire was a Mk IX.

Transports of delight
August 1987

This started life as a crayon drawing on the tablecloth at The Inebriated Newt in Battersea, over dinner with Jonathan Elwes. Charlie Shea-Simonds took over the role of pilot when Jonathan had to dip out because of business commitments.

The CAA took some coaxing, and the locomotive we wanted broke down at the last minute, but it eventually came together, and made a page for the 1987 *One Day for Life* book, raising money for cancer research. Tom Turner drove the train.

The locomotive, a Southern Railway N-class, was built in 1925, and rescued from the Barry scrapyard in 1974. It reopened the pretty Watercress Line in 1977, hauling the inaugural train on 30 April that year.

Sally Henderson turned up to watch, and parked her car with mine in a field. We sat together whilst we waited. People drove past, and turned their heads. Sally giggled, 'They'll think we're having an affair!'

21 December 1986

The Watercress Line

The Watercress Line was closed by British Railways in 1972, and reopened by volunteers in April 1977. It runs between Alresford and Alton in Hampshire.

The T9, built by the London & South Western Railway in 1899, was bashing its way up the steep hill to Four Marks in December 1983. In its day it was known as a 'greyhound', and pulled Queen Victoria's royal train. On this occasion it was getting a bit of help from another, unseen, locomotive.

'Bodmin', built in 1945 by the Southern Railway, was at Alresford station on a frozen December night in 1986. Lighting the scene took two generators, six flash heads, and a lot of manpower to lug it all around. Way after the end of the session, with the frost going white on the tracks, a plaintive voice piped up in the darkness, asking, 'Do I still need to hold onto this?' Celebrating my cleverness in finally having got the whole system to work, I'd totally forgotten one of my helpers, who was still out there somewhere with his fingertips dropping off in the cold, supporting one of the light-stands.

The picture was a straight crib off O. Winston Link, the American advertising photographer who documented the last days of steam on the Norfolk & Western in the 1950s. His book, *Steel, Steam and Stars*, was shot almost entirely at night, and has no equal.

5 December 1983

WEST LONDON
MAGISTRATES COURT

The red dragon in court
6 March 1982

He was wandering around Hammersmith, a bit drunk, so he got arrested at 3 am. He appeared in court the next morning. In his red dragon suit. He had no other clothes. The entire court fell about laughing.

The magistrates fined him £10.

Edward Charles Prosser was a company director up from South Wales for the International at Twickenham. He complained, 'The policeman who arrested me told me he was dragon me off to the station. I don't know why they picked on me...I don't think I was too conspicuous.'

PARTIES FOR SALE

The General Election campaigns of the 1980s were increasingly directed towards the needs of television, with Labour, seeking to catch up in 1983, largely making the running in 1987. Despite losing the 1987 Election, Labour's campaign, masterminded by former advertising man Peter Mandelson, was widely regarded as a triumph. Soft background colours adorned with red roses made press conferences gently reassuring, and softer focus Party broadcasts showed Neil and Glenys Kinnock strolling dreamily through verdant meadows and along clifftops (the sequence was shot near Llandudno in North Wales).

The trend began in 1979, when Gordon Reece, another advertising man, was appointed to oversee the Conservative campaign. Then, as well as in 1983, he was rarely far from Mrs Thatcher's elbow, and was later knighted for his services. The old idea that a party leader goes out to meet the people was effectively dead and buried: in modern elections party leaders go out to meet the television cameras in circumstances that are as controlled as possible. Ironically, the process is aided and abetted by security problems: to minimize the threat of terrorist attack, Mrs Thatcher's programme was rarely announced in advance. Whilst the reasons were understandable, it had the side effect of keeping hostile crowds to a minimum, and allowed the cameras the vision of a prime minister campaigning serenely amidst a grateful populace.

Fortunately things don't always work out quite like that. 1983 had its share of memorable moments, ranging from Mrs Thatcher's helicopter landing in the wrong field at Stoneleigh Abbey, Warwickshire, to the wonderful chaos of Harry Ramsden's chip shop. Peter Dunn described it vividly in his brilliant 1983 *Sunday Times* piece, *Mrs Thatcher's Flying Circus*:

> The climactic shambles came last week at Harry Ramsden's, the country's premier expense account chip shop. Customers who had been given no inkling of the lunch-time invasion, watched saucer-eyed as the awesome weight of the mass media fell upon them. A plate of fish and chips crashed to the floor. One Tory aide shoved hard at a cameraman who was leaning in to get a final shot of the Prime Minister's forkful of food. He fell against a row of colleagues who, in turn, fell domino-fashion onto a table of innocent diners. 'We're just on our way home from holidays', said one elderly couple as the mob struggled and swayed above their heads. 'We only dropped in here for a quiet lunch.' Outside another Tory aide moved among the crowd asking, with mounting desperation, for children to come forward and be served a bag of chips by Mrs Thatcher at the take-away counter'.

I covered the 1983 election as a freelance, and illustrated Carol Thatcher's *Diary of an Election*. Re-read at seven years' distance the book contains a wealth of anecdotal detail not available elsewhere. Carol worked on it night after night, and often nearly all night. It went to press on schedule, the morning after Polling Day.

1987 was *The Independent*'s first election. I was dispatched to cover Labour, alternating between the Kinnock bandwagon and forays elsewhere. Again, the happy accidents abounded, such as the day when the Kinnocks were having a photocall in a South Wales pub, and things were enlivened by one of the television crews crashing off a table which collapsed beneath them. Elsewhere I had a brief encounter with Dennis Skinner, which was memorable for his vitriol, and for subsequently having my car blockaded into a street in a mining village in his Bolsover constituency. There was also the evening when the police at Grimsby tried to arrest Austin Mitchell's wife for 'soliciting' on the quayside, whilst we were photographing on one of the fishing boats. The local girls had been plying their trade when we arrived, and seeing the local MP and his wife, the docks security staff had called the police to have them cleared away. The girls knew full well what was happening, and by the time the police arrived, there was only one woman in sight – Austin's missus.

20 May 1983

3 June 1983

Thatcher in Cornwall
Thatcher at Stoneleigh Abbey

Not entirely in her element in the country. The wellies belonged to Carol, and look far too shiny. They were needed again at Stoneleigh Abbey, when her helicopter's scheduled landing field turned out to be too small, and it was forced to put down in the middle of nowhere.

Gordon Reece rides on the farm cart, just visible in heavy glasses and peaked cap behind the Prime Minister. Ian Gow is to her left, Denis Thatcher is in animated conversation to the right.

Conservative Farm Day tends to be the first stop on the election tour, with a calf or cow to cuddle for the cameras. Neil Kinnock tried sheep, and a horse, in 1987.

Margaret Thatcher in the coach
2 June 1983

Leaving Leicester on 2 June, Margaret Thatcher in deep debate with her advisers, Derek Howe, Michael Spicer, and Roger Boaden. Later that afternoon she abandoned the campaign coach for her car. The coach got lost, and had to find her by following a Weetabix lorry to the factory she was visiting.

Margaret Thatcher in the mirror
9 June 1983

On polling night, in her bedroom in the flat at No 10, preparing to go to the count at Finchley.

To keep herself occupied waiting for the result in 1979, she had turned out clothes drawers. But this time Cecil Parkinson was expected for supper, and had some news about Sarah Keays.

Margaret Thatcher working at No 10 Downing Street
3 June 1983

She was in the 'flat over the shop' at the top of No 10, working on Constituency mail at 12.37 am, after a day which had included touring the Weetabix factory and a lengthy speech-writing conference earlier in the evening, which delayed the picture session until long after midnight. She was up again at 6 am.

Carol placed the shoes neatly by the sofa. Then her mother knocked them over, pointing out that when you kick your shoes off, you rarely line them up, but leave them where they fall.

**Neil Kinnock flying to Birmingham
Neil and Glenys in the pub**

Labour's aircraft in 1987 was a delightful old Viscount, refurbished and operated by British Air Ferries. Known to the Labour press office as 'Red Rose One', it rapidly ended up being dubbed 'Rubber Band One' by the hacks, after displaying a marked reluctance to start up on the first morning of the campaign. But the huge windows and massive leg-room made it a delight to travel on.

Later in the campaign, Neil and Glenys were having a quiet pint in their local, when a television crew filming the event came crashing down as a table collapsed beneath them. Glenys reacted in mock horror.

22 May 1987

Neil Kinnock in the valleys
11 June 1987

Not even the professional image-men could have set this up. It was one of those delightful moments of spontaneity that make elections worth covering.

Neil Kinnock and the Hoover
2 March 1988

Again not quite what the image-makers had in mind. Kinnock was promoting the Welsh Proms, on St David's day in 1988, at the House of Commons.

   I wonder if he grabs a Hoover quite so enthusiastically at home?

GLAMOROUS OLD TROUPERS

Hands coquettishly on hips, like a girl in the playground sneering at her friends, Shirley Bassey is defining her *raison d'être*. "EastEnders, Coronation Street, Emmerdale Farm. Who's interested? I don't want the kitchen sink. Give me *Dallas* and *Dynasty*. I want glamour." The setting is the tearoom of the Ritz and the dress is slinky – a tight black jersey number, split at the side to allow a long, black-stockinged leg to be flourished with full drama. "I want escapism. I want Showbiz."

Everybody knows who Shirley Bassey is. They may never have heard one of her records, but when Joe Longthorne, or any of those impressionists who have made a career perfecting the quiver of her lip, does his Shirley Bassey everyone knows who he means. The two elderly Americans who squeezed past her chair ("Hey Harry, have you signed the bill?") knew who she was. Even the waiters were excited, and they've seen everyone – Clement Freud had just vacated the table next door. Shirley knows that everybody knows who she is. "They are sitting in the lobby of my hotel now, waiting for me. And that frightens me. Not physically, I don't think they want to hurt me, but your life is not your own."

She wears big dark glasses and insists on sitting with her back to the throng, coincidentally facing the mirror. But when the time comes to leave, she can't help going in a showbiz way, negotiating the steps of the Ritz in her towering leapord-skin stilettos like she's on the set of a Busby Berkeley musical. We may be a grandmother, but we can still walk across the tea-room with a girlish flick of the bottom.

Britain's most successful entertainer ("I'm not a pop singer, I hate that word. I'm, I'm, I'm...an Entertainer") was born in Tiger Bay, Cardiff, some time before the war, the seventh child of a mother from northern England and a father from Nigeria. At the time, in a cosmopolitan place, racism was not on the agenda. "The odd kid at school would call me names, but not for long, boy. There was a fighter at the time called Joe 'Kid' Bassey and people used to think we were related. And there was prejudice once when I went for a job. They made out I wasn't any good at arithmetic, which I wasn't, but that wasn't the reason. It was the colour of my skin. But it was not enough to give me a complex, not as it would have been in America. I was glad I was born in Wales."

It was only when she went to America, headlining for the first time, that she came across the curious racial classification with which music there is compartmentalised. "When I opened in Vegas and I sang 'Goldfinger', they all said, 'Why is this black girl singing a white girl's song?' They had never seen me so they thought I was white. They said I had a white voice. I never thought of that. I thought I just had a voice."

Her voice was first noticed in choirs in her home town. It was not long before she had left home and was on the road. Living first in Switzerland and now in Spain, she only really sees Britain when she is here to work. This early departure, she thinks, explains the lack of attachment she has for home, for her Welshness. She doesn't go dewy-eyed when the Marbella orchestra strikes up 'Land of my Fathers'.

"I'd like to be able to say yes I do, but I left so long ago. I'm not really Welsh by blood and I don't speak the language. I love to play Cardiff though, I'm at my very best there." One thing she does go dewy-eyed about, however, is the old show business days. The constituency to which she appeals, the family audience aged from eight to 80 seeking a big-production glamour night out, has contracted. For this she blames the record companies, run by yuppies with no feel for showbiz.

"It's all gone downhill. It's all geared to the kids, the teenyboppers. Nobody's thinking that there are middle-aged people, grannies and mums and 20 to 30-year-olds who want to be entertained. Fortunately I still have an audience, otherwise I would be redundant, I would be a pensioner. A 29-year-old pensioner."

Except for Sting and George Michael ("wonderful voice, writes great songs"), she has little time for most modern pop. "On television they are miming. And these kids spend money on it. Are they aware that they are miming? Which for me, an old trouper, is fraudulent."

Particularly, she has little time for a group called Yello, the Swiss electro-band with whom she collaborated on a single last year, much in the way Liza Minelli and the Pet Shop Boys or Gene Pitney and Marc Almond have. Sadly, it was not as successful a partnership as these others.

"I loved the song, and I think it should have been a hit, but there again the record company did nothing to promote it. The video was too contemporary. It should have been very sophisticated. I mean people saw it and said, 'That's not Shirley Bassey.' Shirley Bassey is glamour, sophistication, sex. But they [Yello] didn't want that, and they were in on everything. They wouldn't let me plug it by myself."

Pop may have disappointed but she has no ambition to move into a more refined orbit. "No. Why disappoint yourself? I am a singer. I would like to do something classical but I can't. It's too late to train. I was once introduced to Sir somebody, David Webb I think, who was in charge of the Opera House. 'God, I see you as a Carmen,' he said. 'If only you could sing opera.' And madam in all innocence said, 'Well why can't I do Carmen?' And he said, 'The key is not your key.' 'Well couldn't we change the key?' And the man had a mouthful of champagne and I thought he was going to have a heart attack."

It was an innocent remark, because for her act songs are tailored to her range. "I hear a song and I tell my musical director what tempo I want it in, and how it's going to end. The ending is very important. The Bassey end."

She had been rehearsing a new song on the way to the Ritz, but didn't know who wrote it.

"I don't know, all I know is Johnny Mathis did it, and it's a lovely song. It doesn't matter who wrote it, I like it."

Frank Sinatra always mentions the writer when he introduces a song, but it is not through generosity, she believes.

"Well, Americans do that. They mention everyone who's had anything to do with the song. It's to rest the voice, you know. Americans love to talk. I just want to get on and do it. You notice how few songs they do. I mean my act is all songs, songs, songs."

Then, after Earl Grey tea and cucumber sandwiches and no holding back on the cake and scones, the perfectly maintained Bassey chassis repaired to the Ritz's dining room for a photo session. It was a wonderful performance, a feast of perfectly choreographed poses and pouts.

"I think I was a stripper in my previous life, or will be in the next," she said, curling her leg round an opulent red curtain. "I'd love to take my clothes off on stage. Everyone goes on about Cher's dresses, showing her navel. I was wearing dresses that showed more than she ever would dare, before she was born. Or perhaps not before she was born."

At the end, the photographer kissed her on both cheeks. "I've wanted to do that all my life," he said. As she left, I shook her hand. "Have a kiss. Don't let the photographer get all the perks."

(Text by Jim White © *The Independent*.)

Inès prepares for her last Chanel show at the Louvre
20 March 1989

Inès de la Fressange was the supreme catwalk model of her generation. She was neither prettier, more sultry, nor technically better than many of her peers. But she was witty, personable, and sublimely aristocratic, and it showed every time she graced the runway.

She left Chanel after disagreements with designer Karl Lagerfeld in the summer of 1989.

She was making-up for her last _prêt-à-porter_ show at the Louvre when I photographed her in March 1989. I met her a couple of nights later at the Gauguin exhibition. 'Theese is my usband!', she trilled, 'Theese is my brother, and' – rounding on her third companion with a triumphant flourish – 'Theese is my lover!'

Quite. Any vacancies?

November 1985

Phil Collins and Bob Hoskins

(How to make a million by losing your hair.)
In 1978 Genesis were on tour in France with their future at stake, because Peter Gabriel had left a few months earlier. Phil Collins had just left his drums for the role of front-man. And he still had some hair. Genesis were always a family band – a sort of Luton Town of the rock world – so Phil Collins' 18-month-old son Simon travelled with them, to the despair of the crew. They wanted excitement. The band kept on going on family outings.

Later, in 1980, I breakfasted with Collins at the Wideopen Holiday Inn near Newcastle, and asked him if he was rich. 'Nah!', he replied. 'You need a top ten album in the States for that'.

Bob Hoskins was filming on a railway bridge near Liverpool Street Station, and after an awful lot of time in the local pub, the picture finally happened at about 4 am. He was instrumental in getting *Mona Lisa* into production. When Neil Jordan, the director, took the script to him, he told him that he'd written the part like 'Biffo' – going round bashing people. They worked on it together, and made a cinema classic.

80

May 1978

March 1985

**Peter Ustinov and
Omar Sharif**

Peter Ustinov was on the set of *Thirteen at Dinner*, one of a series of Agatha Christie films made for television. The picture later appeared on the back cover of Ustinov's 1989 novel *The Disinformer*.

Omar Sharif, witty, courteous and charming, was shooting Alejandro Jodorowski's *The Rainbow Thief* at Shepperton. He co-starred with his friend Peter O'Toole. After the wrap they would go for their customary drinking session. Sharif drank. O'Toole drank milk.

It was their first film together since *Night of the Generals* in 1966. They met some years earlier when David Lean made his masterpiece *Lawrence of Arabia* in 1962. Whiling away the long hours under canvas in the desert, they would sit and speculate on their famous future. Milk-drinking was not on the agenda.

March 1990

9 March 1988

4 September 1987

Sir Anthony Quayle and Albert Finney

Sir Anthony Quayle, whose career read like a history of the British cinema, was tramping the boards again at 74, with Compass Theatre, a travelling company taking classic drama to Blackpool, Brighton and Belfast. He had built a 40-foot ketch to sail the Mediterranean and keep himself amused in retirement, but the lure of the stage was too great. 'You swan off doing a few films and then sail off around the sunny bits of the world. That's no bloody good. Now come on – this is your work, this is your life, this is what you spent 50 years learning. You must pass something on to younger actors.'

His career began in 1931, playing feed to Naylor Grimson, 'The Meanest Man on Earth'. His screen credits included *The Bridge on the River Kwai*, and, like Omar Sharif, *Lawrence of Arabia*. He died in 1989.

Albert Finney was by the canal in Salford, his birthplace.

Shirley Conran
17 October 1983

Millionairess and author – her first novel, *Lace*, was a world-wide best-seller – she was in her bathroom at home in Regent's Park. It was where she did her thinking. Born in 1932, she was 51 when the picture was taken.

Divorced, she complained, 'The great boyfriend crunch is upon us. All over the world, in civilized cities, there's a shortage of fellas. In New York, it's really dreadful. And the ones that are available you wouldn't want to know, they're so smug and self-satisfied.'

Who wants to go to New York anyway?

2 February 1983

Maggie Smith and Diana Rigg

Maggie Smith was in London, and as nervous as a kitten. She was relieved to discover that I was a smoker, and we puffed our way through an enjoyable session, interrupted by cups of coffee and almost any distraction la Smith could think of (she is inventive). Actors and actresses are often uneasy confronted by a still camera, because they are used to winding themselves up to a keen pitch for performance, and the resulting adrenalin kills their nerves before a moving-picture lens. Jack Palance, Peter Ustinov, Harrison Ford and Tim Woodward are others who stand out in memory as having the same love-hate relationship with stills.

Diana Rigg was making herself up at the Ashcroft Theatre in Croydon. She made her name in the 1960s *Avengers* television series, but went on to much greater things. A single-minded woman, she reportedly took an extreme dislike to George Lazenby during the filming of his one James Bond movie, *On Her Majesty's Secret Service*, and primed herself with garlic for their clinches.

24 June 1987

**Timothy Dalton and
Kenneth Branagh**

Kenneth Branagh was shooting *Fortunes of War* for the BBC at Ealing Studios. He'd spent nearly nine months working on it, and he'd climbed the Great Pyramid at Giza. I have also climbed the Great Pyramid at Giza, though, unlike Branagh, it took me nearly nine months to get down again. Actually, I didn't *quite* climb it. I got stuck half way up and came down in the dark with a little help from the film crew I was working with. The trouble with pyramids is that they were built at an angle of 45°, and it doesn't take a degree in applied mathematics to work out that you can't see the bottom from the top. Sensing blood, a crowd of Egyptians gathered, and were mildly disappointed when I jumped off the bottom block suggesting that something very unpleasant should be done with the idiot who designed the thing. Then a Dutch tourist wandered over and asked for an opinion on his camera. I gave him one. A very brief one.

Timothy Dalton was promoting his first Bond film. He wore Rohan pants.

Who's that girl?
(Madonna and Pia Zadora)

The great star of the eighties, and the wannabe.

Shanghai Surprise was a bunfight. Although I had been told in London that the Penns had agreed to publicity, when Richard Tompkins, from *Newsweek*, and I, arrived on set, all hell broke loose. We were thrown out of lunch by Sean Penn, and the next morning he fired the publicist, Chris Nixon. Richard and I made our own arrangements.

Oddly, I was invited back on set a few days later – by Sean Penn – but only after Madonna had departed for Hong Kong.

Pia travelled to St James's Palace in the powder-blue Fabergé Rolls Royce. Her husband, Meshulam Riklis, one of America's richest men, had bought the company a few months earlier. She travelled the world clutching her baby Kady, and always seemed a rather lost little soul. She was once described by Clive James as 'just a very, very ordinary C-grade actress [who] isn't even world-famous in Minneapolis'. Unsurprising, perhaps, when your screen credits include *Santa Claus conquers the Martians*. But I enjoyed her company, and she sang better, live, than she was ever given credit for.

William Boyd on the River Cherwell
9 September 1982

He was a lecturer in English Literature at St Hilda's College, Oxford, and up for the Booker Prize with his second novel, *An Ice Cream War*. We went punting for fun, and talked about his summer touring the USA. He was fascinated by the foibles of American life. Two years later he published *Stars and Bars*, the tale of an Englishman in the States. Daniel Day Lewis starred in the 1990 screen version.

20 June 1979

The Southern Belle and Pam Hogg's punk

Dolly Parton was at the Dorchester in March 1988. She has a gentle Southern charm and flashing wit, completely at odds with her brash image. She grew up in Tennessee, the fourth child of twelve, the daughter of poor farmers. 'I really patterned my look after what they called "the trash" in my hometown. That was the women who were the tramps, and they were bold enough to wear nail polish, bright lipstick and too much make-up, bleach and tease their hair and wear tight clothes. It was romantic, in the fact that they were colourful, and they seemed free.'

Pam Hogg's nightclub punk at the London fashion shows in March 1990 was light years removed in style, if not in spirit. The sleaze on the catwalk was neatly balanced by fistfights amongst the photographers. David Sillitoe of *The Guardian* emerged from the fracas dripping blood. All in a day's work.

The ballet class
22 July 1988

One of those situations where you would need to be blind and dead from the neck upwards to avoid shooting something good. There were probably more awards from this one photocall than from any other in years: it was a situation made in heaven, though not quite what the Kirov's PR company had in mind. By the time their official session got under way, I was sitting on a balcony overlooking the scene, having a cup of coffee with actor Nat Parker, with whom I'd worked on *Piece of Cake*. 'Shouldn't you be down there?', he asked. I grinned. 'No.'

1 July 1984

Lord Denning
Princess Anne

Hat people. Lord Denning, former Master of the Rolls, was on a walk near his home in Hampshire.

Princess Anne was at a scouts' presentation at Leeds Castle, Kent. The picture, taken for the *Sunday Times*, was never published.

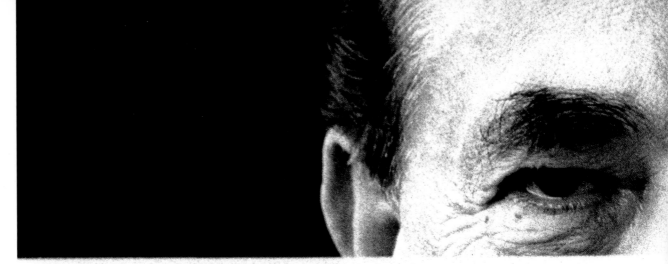

Robert Maxwell at The Daily Mirror

14 July 1984

Publisher Robert Maxwell achieved his long-standing desire to own a national newspaper by buying the Mirror Group in July 1984. That gave him four in one go. He founded, and closed, the *London Daily News* in 1987, and then started *The European*, a weekly, in May 1990.

Born in Czechoslovakia, he served in the British Army during the war, winning a Military Cross.

DAILY Mirror

DON'T LOSE IT AGAIN

Vote for them

VOTE

MA
ON

FORWARD WITH BRITAIN ★ ─ 17p

Sunday, July 16, 1984

FORWARD
WITH

'My

THE Mirror Group newspap-ers have changed owner-ship. Their policies will not change.

I am proud to be the proprietor of this group of publications which holds such an important position in the life of the nation.

I certainly hope to make the papers more efficient and thereby

● TH
his
the Da
the Mi
history
and th

**Tobacco worker
at Piedmont**
February 1980

She was bringing in the
ripe leaves from the
fields on my cousin's
farm at Bindura. She
still lives there now,
and has a young family.